saints who shaped the church

Saints Who Shaped the Church

Stories and sermons by Jerry L. Schmalenberger
Musical notes by Larry Christensen
Edited by Ellen Hanusa

C.S.S. Publishing Co., Inc.
Lima, Ohio

SAINTS WHO SHAPED THE CHURCH

Library of Congress Cataloging-in-Publication Data

Schmalenberger, Jerry L. 1934-
Saints who shaped the church.

1. Christian biography — Sermons. 2. Children's sermons. 3. Object-teaching. I. Christensen, Larry, 1946- . II. Hanusa, Ellen. III. Title.
BR1700.2.S35 1987 270'.092'2 [B] 86-28395
ISBN 0-89536-856-0

7815 / ISBN 0-89536-856-0 PRINTED IN U.S.A.

Table of Contents

One

Augustine, Defender of the Faith

Two

Francis of Assisi: A Faith for Every Day

Three

Martin Luther: The Shape of Grace

Four

John Calvin, God's Man

Five

John Wesley: Religion of the Heart

Six

William Booth and His Hallelujah Army

Seven

Mother Teresa and the Dying Poor

Eight

Musical Notes

Children's Object Lesson

Augustine, Defender of the Faith

Object: *large lump of modeling clay*

Good morning, boys and girls. Today I brought this lump of clay to this church service. It comes from the toy box at our house. I'll bet many of you use clay at your house or at school.

What I like to do best with this clay is make something nice like a house, a car, a castle, or some letters. Then I like to take what I made and mash it together, like I'm doing now, and reshape it into something else.

It's the same clay, but it takes a different shape.

Over the next few weeks we're going to talk about great leaders who did the same thing to the Christian church. They took the stuff which is the church and reshaped it so that it appeared differently.

We'll talk about "reformers." The word *reform* means to give new shape to the same stuff, to re-form. That's what John Calvin, John Wesley, William Booth, Martin Luther, Mother Teresa, and others have done over the years.

As God needed to give new shape to his church so that he could continue to bless his people, these reformers helped reshape the church into the needed new form.

Today we'll talk about one of those reformers, John Calvin. He reshaped the church so that we all might know God's will in our lives. He reformed the church so we could discover what God would have us do in our community and in our own individual lives each day.

I hope you'll remember over the next few weeks what it means to be a reformer. A reformer is one who re-shapes the church, just like I have done with this lump of clay.

Augustine, Defender of the Faith

There is a way of looking at the personal stories of certain women and men to learn of the richness and the potential of human life lived by the grace of God. We are going to do that over the next weeks in this series of sermons we have chosen to name "Saints Who Shaped the Church."

The people we will consider convey something of the breadth of Christian history. They are a rich assortment of young and old, learned and ignorant, people of action and people of thought, whose common denominator is simply that the grace of God worked mightily within them.

We will consider:

- *John Calvin,* God's man for the time, and how he shaped the Reformed church;
- *John Wesley,* who saw religion as issues of the heart, and his shaping of the Methodist church;
- *William Booth,* his deep concern for the soul's safety, and how he shaped the Salvation Army.
- *Martin Luther,* his lifting up of God's grace gives new shapes for an old church.
- *Mother Teresa,* a contemporary Roman Catholic nun, and how her Christ-like concern for the poor and dying has shaped compassionate ministries around the world.

These saints who shaped the church have, indeed, given the world examples of human lives inspired by the power of God.

Today, we will talk about Augustine, defender of the faith. He struggled with his own sin and shaped the theology of

Christianity.

Augustine was born in North Africa on November 13, 354, a little over 300 years after Christ's death on the cross. His father was a pagan. His mother was a Christian, later named St. Monica in the Roman church. He abandoned what Christianity he had and took on a concubine for fifteen years. For nine years, he embraced a religion called Manichaeism.

Then, he went on to Rome and taught rhetoric. From there, he traveled to Milan, where he was influenced by St. Ambrose. In fact, he was baptized into the Christian faith by St. Ambrose at the Easter Vigil in 387, after finding the Scripture verse, Romans 13:13-14:

> *Let us conduct ourselves properly, as people who live in the light of day — no orgies or drunkenness, no immorality or indecency, no fighting or jealousy. But take up the weapons of the Lord Jesus Christ, and stop paying attention to your sinful nature and satisfying its desires.*

Augustine went back to Africa and opened a kind of monastery at Tagaste, where he and his Christian friends lived. On a visit to Hippo, the people compelled the bishop to ordain him. At age 42 he became a bishop of the See of Hippo (a region of North Africa), and for 35 years he served in that capacity in God's church.

As bishop, he had to deal with three major heresies. As so often is true in Christianity, the majority of his writings opposed what he did not believe. That shaped his theology and the theology of early Christianity.

The truths he discovered and wrote about were 1) sin is the result of free will and imperfect creatures, 2) evil does not stop at the church doors, and 3) as a member of the human race, it is only by God's grace that we are saved.

The Manicheans claimed there was an evil god or power which was eternally opposed to the good god. Augustine defended the essential goodness of all creation. He claimed evil is the product of free will and our own imperfect nature.

Augustine knew first-hand! He had tried out the lust of the flesh and lived a self-indulgent life, right up to his baptism. His writings, *The Confessions of Augustine,* graphically portray the kind of hedonistic life in which he tried to find fulfillment and satisfaction, but to no avail.

In his Confessions he wrote these words: "Solitude was more suitable for weeping, so I moved far enough away that even his presence could not embarrass me . . . After this manner I spoke to you: 'How long, O Lord, how long?' . . . Why is there not this moment an end to my wickedness?

> *"So I was speaking and weeping in the bitter contrition of my heart, when suddenly I heard from a neighboring house a voice, 'Take up and read, take up and read.'*
>
> *". . . in silence I read that passage on which my eyes first fell: 'Let us conduct ourselves properly, as people who live in the light of day — no orgies or drunkenness, no immorality or indecency, no fighting or jealousy. But take up the weapons of the Lord Jesus Christ, and stop paying attention to your sinful nature and satisfying its desires.' "*
>
> — *Confessions,* VIII, 12 translation, P.H.B. based on the translation of Edward B. Pusey.

These words have a lot to say to us who live 1,600 years after the "defender of the faith." It is always a struggle to be a Christian. If we are not struggling, we probably don't yet have the correct concept of what it means to be a disciple of Jesus Christ.

Those evil desires of our imperfect nature tempt and con vince us, also:

- that lust to possess others sexually;
- that greed to get and keep all we can;
- that self-centered ego which tells us to tramp on others to get ahead;
- that lack of self-esteem which drives us to be critical of everyone else;
- and that which our American way of life encourages: "If it feels good, do it."

Augustine's and St. Paul's struggle is our struggle: "Let us conduct ourselves properly, as people who live in the light of day — . . . and stop paying attention to your sinful nature and satisfying its desires."

Our Human Nature Says:	God Says:
• Cheat if no one will know.	• You and I will know.
• We must keep up with the neighbors.	• Pride goes before a fall.
• Everyone else is doing it.	• You are my family and that means self-discipline.
• Get wealth any way you can and keep it for yourself — that's happiness.	• The real joy of life is what you give away and share with others.
• Get even no matter what — that's what it means to be a man.	• Love those who persecute you.
	• Love your enemies and you will be blessed.

St. Augustine would condemn any practice of faith which simply endorses what the masses want. He would want to talk to Christians who join the church and fail to experience a real change in their lives, except for that certain respectability they feel because they attend worship occasionally.

Usually we want the faith to put a stamp of approval on what we as sinful humans want, rather than what our creator God intended for us.

Augustine would remind us that evil is still with us through our free will, our humanness. He would tell us the struggle goes on until we join the other imperfect saints on the opposite side of that glorious resurrection.

An executive was having a bad day. He decided to cheer himself up by calling home and talking to his wife. The maid answered the telephone. "I'd like to speak to my wife." "She's having an affair with the butler and can't talk to you now," she said. "Get my gun and shoot the both of them!" he ordered. There was a long silence on the line. Finally, the maid came back to the phone. She said, "I shot them both and, to be of help to you, I threw both their bodies in the swimming pool." "Swimming pool? We don't have a swimming pool! Is this 278-0246?"

Our lives are imperfect, and we *do* deserve to be shot. We all need to hear Augustine's favorite Scripture: "Let us conduct ourselves properly, as people who live in the light of day — . . . and stop paying attention to your sinful nature and satisfying *its* desires."

Evil does not stop at the church doors. The heresy of the Donatist compelled Augustine to rethink his definition of the church. He finally came to the right conclusion, that "The church is holy because of her *purposes* and not her *members.*" Further, he believed, "She contains within her fold both good persons and evil."

The church is not, as some believe, a place for the display of good people. Within the congregation we find all the symptoms of being human that we find anywhere else. We gather because we know we are imperfect and sinful. We come to celebrate that God still gives us blessed forgiveness.

Our relationship to each other is not a demand for perfection, but rather it is an expectation of undeserved forgiveness.

There is neither a perfect pastor unscarred by mistakes, nor a perfect member who has discipleship accomplished.

Like ill people who gather in hospitals and uneducated people in schools, we sinners gather in churches. Only Christ is holy and perfect. Only his word and sacraments are his pure, undiluted presence in the world.

This is the reason no one political candidate or party can be designated "of God" and the other of "the evil one."

In fact, it seems clear that the human organization of the church so blunders and limps along with its human organization that it would have died out years ago had it not been "of

God."

This has a lot to say about our behavior as church members. *Of course,* you can easily find many reasons not to give your offering. *Of course,* you can find hundreds of hypocrites in the congregation, beginning with you and me. *Of course,* you can find serious errors in any pastor's attempt at ministry. *Of course,* you can find better-run, less offensive, more attractive "entertainment' than here in the church where sinners gather. That's because we need to be better and desperately need God's help and guidance to do it. Jesus knew that, and he told the church members of his day, "Why do you look at the speck in your brother's eye and pay no attention to the log in your own eye?" (Matthew 7:3)

As members of the human race, only God's grace saves us. If that idea, put forth by Augústine, has a familiar ring to it, remember that Martin Luther was an Augustinian friar. He became a monk in the very order that Augustine founded, and there he learned his basic theology.

Augustine called for a radical change in what was called Pelagianism. He taught: we, by our birth into the human race, inherit a moral disease — from these evils we can be saved only by God's grace. It is not our choice. The Almighty elected and chose us to be the saved and part of his redeemed family. (This idea of predestination and election profoundly shaped the belief of John Calvin, about whom we will hear more later in this series.)

Dean Fischer at Grand View College here in Des Moines tells a humorous story about graduation day last spring. He was amazed to see, complete with robe and mortar board, one of the Kuwaiti students from Grand View in line for graduation. The young lad had not completed his requirements, but was going to go up and get his diploma anyway. The dean literally had to pull him out of line. In that part of the world, the Kuwaiti think that everything can be negotiated and bargained for.

We are like that Kuwaiti student. We do not deserve the

award by our actions and grades, but God lets us be here anyway.

Our whole attitude now is not one of pride that we have accomplished a religious and moral victory. Rather, we are amazed, astonished, and thankful that God chose us. When we eventually understand that idea, how our attitudes toward church, and even God, change! We do not "do him a favor" by being here. He is not flattered that we select him over the golf course, the football game, or an outing at the lake.

Another passage in Romans reads, "But God has shown us how much he loves us — it was while we were still sinners that Christ died for us! We rejoice because of what God has done through our Lord Jesus Christ, who has now made us God's friends." (Romans 5:8, 11b)

How this changes our attitude toward each other, our church, and its ministry and mission!

- No more resentment when the church asks for help, be it with our time or our money.
- No more excuses when the church offers opportunity to learn and mature further in our faith.
- No more anger when mistakes are made by pastors, staff, and council.
- No more timidity when the opportunity comes to serve and witness to our faith.

Humility replaces pride, gentleness replaces meanness, and sincerity replaces hypocrisy.

Augustine, defender of the faith, was one of the great teachers of the church and a great Christian thinker. Both Roman Catholics and Protestants acknowledge his importance as a theologian and shaper of the church.

He taught us that:

1. Sin is the result of free will and imperfection.
2. Evil does not stop at the church doors.
3. As a member of the human race, it is only by God's grace that we are saved.

All this came from his own early life of debauchery, and from God, who spoke to him in Romans 13: "Let us conduct ourselves properly, as people who live in the light of day . . . take up the weapons of the Lord Jesus Christ, and stop paying attention to your sinful nature and satisfying its desires."

Augustine established his monastic rule of St. Augustine. During the Vandals' seige of Hippo in 430, he was seized with a fever and died on August 28, 430 AD, the date on which he is now commemorated. Truly, he was a saint who shaped the church.

Children's Object Lesson

Saint Francis of Assisi: a Faith for Every Day

Object: *a picture of a dog, cat or rabbit*

Good morning, boys and girls. Do you like this picture of a special pet? This is a dog named Heinrick who lives at our house. We love Heinrick very much, and he's certainly a part of our family.

I'll bet many of you have pets at your house. Tell me about your pet and what your pet's name is.

Today we're talking about a Christian who lived a long time ago and whose name was Francis. Francis lived in an Italian town named Assisi.

One of the things that Francis taught Christians, and we still remember, is that God loves animals like he loves people. Francis never thought he was better than an animal. He was always very careful not to hurt any of God's creation, including all the birds and animals. He taught that because God made them too, and they were part of the world that God gives to us, we must love and care for them in a very gentle and God-like way.

There's a story about Francis that one time a very bad wolf was hurting people in a whole little town. It was attacking the animals and people in this little community. The story goes that St. Francis, without any protection or weapons, went out and tamed the animal, and now artists even draw pictures of that same wolf lying at St. Francis' feet like a gentle lamb.

There's another story that tells of all the birds coming to the house and staying there all night the night that Francis died. The story goes that the birds sang because they wanted the people to know that their very best friend had died, and that his life was a beautiful story, just as beautiful as their songs.

I hope you can remember Francis as a saint who shaped the church and who taught us to love all creation, including all the birds and animals, because they also belong to God.

Francis of Assisi: a Faith for Every Day

A Prayer attributed to St. Francis

Lord, make us instruments of your peace.
Where there is hatred, let us sow love;
where there is injury, pardon;
where there is discord, union;
where there is doubt, faith;
where there is despair, hope;
where there is darkness, light;
where there is sadness, joy.
Grant that we may not so much seek
to be consoled as to console;
to be understood as to understand;
to be loved as to love.
For it is in giving that we receive;
it is in pardoning that we are pardoned; and
it is in dying that we are born to eternal life.

When the Reformation was the hottest, about 1530, Phillip Melancthon, Luther's best scholar and spokesperson, wrote in defense of the Augsburg Confession about a Roman Catholic saint named Francis. He called him "Holy Father whose faith in God affected every day of life." More than 800 years after his birth, Christians share Francis, digging him up from the grave to probe his life, hoping that his power of reconciliation still hovers about his remains.

The *Oxford Dictionary of the Christian Church* tells us that Francis was the son of a rich merchant who became dissatisfied with his worldly life. On a pilgrimage to Rome he exchanged clothes with a beggar and spent the day begging.

When he returned to Assisi, after being disowned by his father, he devoted himself to repairing a ruined church. In 1208, Francis heard read in church his Lord's words bidding his disciples to leave all (Matthew 10:7-19) and understood them as a personal call to save souls.

He soon gathered a band of followers. He drew up a simple rule of life based on sayings from the Gospels for himself and this group. In 1212, his ideals were accepted by St. Clare, who founded a similar society for women. In 1221, he founded the Tertiaries. These people wanted to adopt his lifestyle as far as was compatible with normal life.

Francis received the gift of the stigmata (the five wounds of Christ) in 1224. His generosity, his simple faith, his passionate devotion to God and people, his love of nature, and his deep humility have made him one of the most cherished saints in modern times.

Let's see what this holy man has to teach us in our day. He certainly holds for us a model of a Christ-like attitude toward wealth and poverty.

A fourteenth century document tells how Francis was elected "King of the Revels" in his village. His friends gave him a free hand to spend what he liked for a feast. After the feast, they were going through the streets. All of a sudden the Lord touched his heart. His companions looked back and saw that he was transformed into another man. He explained that he was thinking of wooing the noblest, richest, and most beautiful bride ever seen. The bride was none other than the form of true religion which he embraced. It was noble, rich, and beautiful in its poverty.

Francis was already a benefactor of the poor, but from this time on he resolved never to refuse alms to anyone who begged in God's name.

"If a poor person begged of him when he was far from home, he would always give him money, if possible; when he had none to give — he would give his belt buckle, or — taking off his shirt, give it to a beggar for the love of God."

(Legend of Three Companions, ca. 1325)

So when he was in his early twenties, Francis began a new life. He called poverty his "mother, his bride, and his lady fair."

There is a big difference between the way Francis interpreted the words of Jesus in Matthew 10 and the way we have traditionally heard them from our lecterns. The instructions for his disciples were very specific: "Do not carry any gold, silver, or copper money in your pockets; do not carry a beggar's bag for the trip or an extra shirt or shoes or a walking stick." (Matthew 10:9-10)

How in the world should we live in our affluent culture? You have heard me tell you of my struggle with this question, and I am hopeful that you also are struggling with it. Jesus said to sell all you have and give it to the poor; he told that to a rich young man. Paul advised a restrained lifestyle lived in moderation.

The Church recalls the lives of many who live with minimal comforts in order to share their goods with others. That is a far cry from the way we must coax and beg members to make out pledge cards for the coming year! And those pledges are such a tiny percentage of our entire income!

Since we cannot easily sell out and give up, perhaps Saint Francis had the answer — *to share,* and in large quantity.

When Francis was inspired to donate money to rebuild the church, he took expensive cloth from his merchant father's stock and sold it for the necessary cash. When his father hauled him before the bishop for retribution, Francis stripped himself naked before the assembly. He donned a poor man's garb of sackcloth, and when it was torn, he mended it with yet another ragged piece of sackcloth.

The church has always seen in the life of the poor a sign of God's grace. The "poor of God" is one Hebraic expression for those whom God will save. Mary's "Magnificat" (Luke 1) includes the promise that God will care for the hungry and lowly who receive his Gospel. Today, in the twentieth century, the issue of world poverty is still with us. Our present political tendency to close off help to the poor in America makes it even more important that the non-profit part of our society — like our congregation — take up the clothing and feeding of our land.

Surely Francis' embrace of the poor calls us to embrace the poor of our world. Not only the world's hungry — as if starving people are not enough to care for! We must also be concerned about the lepers whom Francis embraced, the social outcasts, refugees and morally repulsive — the list is endless. The mission derelicts, the transients who come through town, ex-offenders, those locked in jails, those on welfare whom we think do not deserve help, those who are out of work. If Francis teaches us anything, it is to care for the poor here and around the world.

Francis also witnesses to the call that came from the open Bible. St. Francis' first biographer writes that during the several years of conversion, his encounter with the Gospel was decisive. He saw in the Scripture a direct bearing on his daily life. He listened and then went out and did. This is another point where we Christians and this saint agree. Our authority is the Scripture.

We also believe that the Scripture makes radical changes in our lives if we take it seriously. What Francis heard proclaimed, he obeyed literally, as few Christians before or since have done. If Jesus commanded it, Francis followed it.

In another famous story, Bernard, a neighbor from Assisi, came to Francis for spiritual direction. Francis said, pointing to the Bible: "Just open the book." The three verses Bernard read were ones which advised him to "sell what he had, take nothing for the journey, and to deny himself." Bernard, once a noble, became Francis' first companion.

Although Francis was attracted to contemplative prayer, he believed that his primary call was to preach the open book to the world. He did, indeed, teach us to treasure and follow the Scripture. Just think what that would mean if we would:

- Love one another.
- Love our enemies.
- Not store up our riches here.
- Tithe all our income.
- Always witness to our faith.
- Make disciples of all people.

That is radical stuff, and Francis said that we ought to *live it* in the world! It comes from the Scripture, and he discovered it there.

Francis also called all living things his friends. A legend tells about a wolf that was troubling and ravaging a town. The wolf was attacking animals and people in the little community. Saint Francis went out without any weapons and tamed the animal, which was described as lying at his feet like a lamb. When Francis died, legend has it that the birds gathered on the roof of the house and sang all night. The city watchman told the story.

There are all kinds of stories about St. Francis and the animals. According to Bonaventure, Francis' compassion bound him to the creatures of nature. "It was loving compassion . . . which led him to devote himself humbly to his neighbor, and enabled him to return to the state of primal innocence by restoring man's harmony with the whole of creation." The words that Bonaventure used for compassion include love, devotion, reverence, kindness. Francis' humility before God kept him from exerting superiority over creatures — animal or human.

We are incarnational people. Christians believe that God became incarnate and took on human flesh in the person of Jesus. By the merging of the divine and the human, all created order is viewed differently. All other people and creatures are also God's, and we ought to treat them that way.

We value nature; we value other humans. This idea constantly reminds us how we are to view other denominations. We are sisters and brothers in Christ. We are never to be haters of another group or family of God. We have a common purpose and a common Savior and Creator. But we are much more than tolerated friends. St. Francis learned this truth from Christ. We are to be friends with all creation, with each other, and with our God.

Francis is a reminder of the shape of the church:

- We share Christ on the cross.
- We share the Good News of the Scripture.
- We share the call to discipleship.
- We share our baptism.
- We share our Sacrament at the Altar.

The poor of the world have been given to us to embrace; the fragmented body of Christ needs to be unified so our witness is more effective.

Not only did St. Francis teach us a Christ-like attitude toward wealth and poverty, a call from an open Bible, a befriending of all God's people and creation, but also that his sign is our sign, too: the sign of the cross.

"We can glory in the cross," said Francis to Brother Leo. With the sign of the cross, Francis summarized his inspiration for life, the sustenance of his vitality, the focus of his commitment.

Francis' subjection to the cross had begun long ago in the empty church of St. Damian, when he thought that the lips of Christ spoke to him about his mission. Francis had seen a vision of the living Christ; he heard the cross and obeyed.

When he taught his companions how to pray, he taught them to first offer the Lord's Prayer, and then this prayer of the cross:

> *"We adore you, Lord Jesus Christ, here and in all your churches and in the whole world, and we bless you, because by your holy cross you have redeemed the world."*

We Christians hold as central the theology of the cross taught by another saint who shaped the church, Saint Paul. Rather than a morbid threat to "get saved or burn in hell," our approach is to gather at the foot of the cross with other sinners and join their precious response to God's gift of grace and forgiveness. The cross joins us together as blood brothers and sisters and family. Central to our life's existence is the cross and its glory.

On September 14, 1224, the Feast of the Holy Cross, Francis was on retreat alone and fasting. His friend called out to him and got no response. The little brother went to check on him. The brother found Francis lying prostrate, still dazed by the vision of the Crucified which he had experienced. Francis discovered the marks of Christ's crucifixion on his hands and feet and side. According to a recent biography, the rest of his life he tried to cover up these marks with clothing. Those who laundered his clothing used cold water to remove the blood from his wounds, called the stigmata.

A saint who shaped the church with a religion for every day: St. Francis, one whom we can all share. He tells us:

- His sign is ours, too — the cross.
- We should see all of God's creation as friends.
- Our call comes from the Scripture.
- We must have a Christ-like attitude toward wealth and poverty.

Children's Object Lesson

Martin Luther: the Shape of Grace

***Objects:** a law book and a Bible with a chain around it*

Good morning, boys and girls. Today we will talk about another saint who shaped the church. His name was Martin Luther. He lived in Germany almost 500 years ago. He was the greatest reformer of all time. On hallowed eve, which we now call Halloween, he nailed a notice on the doors of a village church and began the Reformation.

I brought two things that tell us about Martin Luther. The first is a law book. The second is this Bible with a chain around it.

The law book illustrates that Martin Luther started to study law at the University of Leipzig. One day, when he was walking home from the university through a storm, lightning struck very near to him. Martin was terribly frightened. He prayed to St. Anne and asked that if she saved him, he would become a pastor. She did, and he did. Luther became a priest and professor at the little town of Wittenberg, Germany.

It was at Wittenberg that Luther discovered something new about the Christian church. Thus he is one of the saints who reshaped it. He discovered that people needed the words of the Bible to guide their lives.

Until that time, the Bible was in a language (Latin) that few people spoke. For that reason, the Bible wasn't understood. Just think, most people couldn't read the Bible like we do.

I put a chain around this Bible to show you how Bibles were chained to walls back then. It's much like the big phone directories which are chained to walls now. Because there was no printing press and everything had to be copied by hand, Bibles were very expensive. So they chained them to the walls so people would not carry them away. But the fact that the Bible was in a different language really chained it. Church members couldn't read or understand God's Word.

Martin Luther translated the Bible into the German language for the German people. He made it easy for them to read and understand it. About the same time, the printing press came along. The Bible could be printed more cheaply, and everybody could have their own Bible. Because of this, Luther is considered the father of the German language.

What's more important to us is that he shaped a large part of the church by unchaining the Bible and putting it in the hands of all the people.

I hope you can remember these things about Martin Luther:

He was studying law and promised God that he would be a pastor when God spoke to him through lightning. He shaped the Christian church by making God's Word in the Holy Bible available to every person.

Martin Luther: the Shape of Grace

Martin Luther died in the upstairs bedroom of a little house in the town of Eisleben, Germany. He had been taken there from St. Andrew's church across the street where he preached his last sermon. On February 18, 1546, he died. From the window of that little East German bedroom you can see St. Anne's church, where he was baptized at the age of one day, and the house where he was born.

Hans and Margaret Luder were on their way to Mansfield to look for work in the copper mines. As they traveled through Eisleben, they had to stop for their son's birth on November 10, 1483. The next day, November 11, St. Martin's day, they took their firstborn to the parish church for baptism. They gave him the name of the day.

Then it was on to Mansfield where Hans became a prosperous businessman. Martin was a good scholar and studied to be a lawyer.

In July, 1505, returning to the university from a visit home, he unexpectedly encountered death. He was 21 and a student at the University of Erfurt. There was a terrible storm. Lightning struck nearby, and Martin fell to the ground. In his fright he called out to the patron saint of miners, "St. Anne, help me! I will become a monk." She did, and he did!

Luther entered the monastery at Erfurt, was ordained, and became a professor at a new little university at Wittenberg. The year was 1512. He was a master at Latin, Greek, and Hebrew. He began giving lectures on the Bible.

Lecturing from the original language of the Scriptures opened a whole new world to him and caused him to seriously question the shape of the Christian church in his day. By 1517, he was ready to debate the issues with the scholars. So, on All Saints' Eve, Hallowed Eve, October 31, which we call Halloween, he placed his 95 arguments, called theses, on the village bulletin board: the Castle Church doors in Wittenberg.

That's the place and time. And Luther was the person, who more than any other person, re-formed the Christian church.

Had it not been for a couple of things brewing at that time, the incident would have remained a "tempest in a teapot." It would have been just a scholarly debate in Latin in some lecture hall among the educated elite of the day. But Gutenberg had invented the printing press, and German printers were looking for something to publish. The political mood of the day called for an overthrow of the Holy Roman Empire's control. Nationalism was running high. Those 95 theses, translated into the language of the people, spread like wildfire. The battle of the Reformation was on for good. The floodgates of God's grace had not been opened this wide for the last 1,000 years. The shape of the Christian church would never be the same.

Martin Luther actually "re-formed" the church into its *earlier* form. He called for the more original shape of Christianity in three areas: Bible, priesthood, and salvation.

Luther asked that the Scriptures be placed in the hands of the people and in their language so that their lives could be shaped by it. He claimed everyone was a priest in God's sight and had a ministry to carry on in the world. He held up before the people of his day the fact that we are saved by God's gift of grace, not by living the life of perfection that would earn it for us.

You can still see the Augustinian monastery of the black friars at Erfurt where Luther tried in every way to appease God. You can go up to the second floor and see the cell where he lived and where one time he flogged himself all night long, almost to the point of death, in order to gain God's favor.

Then, Luther discovered it in the Scriptures, and it changed the shape of his faith and our church: "But by the free gift of God's grace all are right with him through Christ Jesus, who sets them free." (Romans 3:24)

The saddest part of Martin Luther's story is these new, exciting shapes of the church have become old, stagnant, and bloated. We desperately need a new re-forming of the church today. We need another Luther, Wesley, Calvin, or Booth right now and in this place. We need bold thinkers and protestors in direct touch with the Almighty God to call for new shape in our church now.

I have had the profound privilege of traveling to Wittenberg, East Germany, several times. I have worshiped in the Stadt Kirche (city church) where Luther was parish pastor his entire ministry. A Pastor Haas has given up his West German citizenship in order to serve that little group of people now.

When I visited that church and greeted the congregation a week before the 450th anniversary of the Reformation in 1967, I was shocked by the tiny little group that met there. The church could hold 700 worshipers. But on that Sunday morning, only 27 were seated there. Most of them had come from America with me. The remainder were very old people. The church was mausoleum-like, dark, damp, and dreary. Everything seemed antique, unused, and musty. An oppressive communist government shadowed our every move as we made our visit.

Four-hundred-fifty years of trying to keep the church the same as when Luther was there had taken its toll. Many years of being the famous church had stultified the congregation and any mission and ministry it might have once held.

It was an unpleasant experience to see how stifled and nearly dead the Lutheran religion was at the very place it began.

We as a congregation have something to learn from this. That which was exciting and new, and for which people laid their lives on the line, had been organized, commercialized, stilted, and downright boring. It could happen here.

Think what it would mean to our own congregation if we

took seriously those three shapes Luther insisted on in his day. Imagine what it would mean if all our members who had a Bible read it regularly and knew its contents. Think of the impact on our community if all 3,500 members here took their baptism seriously and carried out their own ministries in the world. Consider the joy evidenced in our worship and our stewardship emphasis if we all believed in the wonderful gift of God's grace as proclaimed by Martin Luther.

Any congregation which could re-form into that shape again would double in size, minister to thousands around it, have an abundance of offerings to share, and probably be on the cover of *Time* magazine within the year.

Put very bluntly, we have no right to use the name "protestant" in 1985 unless:

We are deeply versed and directed by the Scriptures.

We are in the world every day doing our own ministry.

We are just downright thrilled with God's free gift of grace and salvation so that we share it with everyone who will hold still to listen.

Often, however, we are like the Christians in Luther's day. We are Bible-ignorant. We expect the preacher to do our ministry. And we are plain stingy with grace. We still try to earn our salvation and carry an unnecessary burden of guilt.

Martin Luther pointed out the abuses in the church in his day and called for a re-forming of Christianity. Not only did the world's largest protestant denomination grow from his life, but he gave a new shape to Christianity. It's a free way. It's a way centered on personal faith. It's a way of individual responsibility.

At the Diet of Worms in 1521, Luther took his famous stand. When asked to denounce what he had written calling for a change in the church and of Christianity, he stood before the emperor and said: "Here I stand, I can do no other, God help me. Amen."

We ought to be in the lineage of this reformer, calling for continual re-forming and changing of the church. We ought to be a dynamic organization adjusting to whatever time and geography in which we find ourselves. We ought to make relevant the good news to whatever the contemporary situation.

This will mean new liturgies, new books of worship, new social statements, new translations of the Bible, new positions for the altar, new ways of administering and scheduling sacraments, new mergers and organizations. While the content and core remain the same, the shape the church takes continues to be effective in whatever the day and situation.

We ought to be ashamed of ourselves if we use the names Lutheran and protestant and yet try to keep everything the way it was when we were growing up. We must never try to freeze this dynamic church in any age or place. We who are in the lineage of the Reformation have abuses to point out and change to work for as well. We must be 20th century protestors. It's a different age now. We must find ways to hold up the cross of Jesus Christ for this time.

We now live in an age when one angry command can start a nuclear war which will obliterate the world. We must work to disarm that ever-threatening monster.

We live in a time when travel and communication make it a horrible sin to allow a few to have so much and so many to have so little. We must work to bring about change, a new sense of world community, and a system that feeds and opens up communication among all the earth's people.

Whenever the bureaucracy of the organized church aggrandizes and proliferates itself at the expense of caring about and ministering to the world's less privileged, we need to protest and cause another reformation. And when church mergers take place, we must make sure the bureaucracy of the church remains lean and effective for mission and ministry.

There are evils out in the world which must be held up for correction: racism, sexism, institutional violence, militarism, abuse of people. Martin Luther would argue that we should confront injustice wherever we find it and in whatever form it takes. He would say we should use God's word to bring about justice and change.

Luther's Reformation gave the church many new shapes. The sanctity of marriage for a pastor and the institution of the church parsonage began when Luther married Katherine Von Bora, a Roman Catholic nun. This story is delightful, because he spirited her and a number of other nuns out of the convent and then found husbands for them in the Lutheran clergy.

Luther gave us worship in our own language and congregational lay people taking part in the worship by singing hymns and liturgy and participating in the service itself.

Martin Luther was probably responsible for burning down more German homes than any other person. He thought that evergreen trees ought to be brought inside the house and lit with candles. We have substituted safe electric Christmas tree lights for candles, but we follow in his tradition nonetheless.

I have held in my hands the Bible from the desk Luther used to teach and preach. I turned that book's old brittle pages to John's gospel, chapter 8:31 and read the words again: "You will know the truth, and the truth will set you free." In large letters across the margin in Luther's own hand was written, "free indeed!" This young man struggled with sin, guilt, and churchly abuses — and found the church. He was freed. So may we be as well.

It broke Luther's heart that his protest brought about a split between Protestant and Roman Catholic Christians. He didn't want to split the church. Rather he wanted to re-shape and re-form it keeping the unity of the body of Christ catholic.

Luther would be pleased with the mood of our day. He would like the new direction in 1985 of seeking out unity of purpose and mission again. We no longer are "Catholic-haters" as some have been. We recognize each other as true brothers and sisters in Christ — one in baptism. We look forward to the time when we can not only join hands in our ministry, mission, and baptism, but can kneel at God's altar to receive the sacrament of Holy Communion. This would best show our oneness.

According to Louis Cranach's paintings, those Saxon Germans were homely people. But one born November 10, 1583, in Eisleben, Germany, to Hans and Margaret Luder gave a beautiful new shape to the Christian church. His Reformation made the church Bible-centered and everyone a priest. It filled the church with God's grace and forgiveness. The form of the church wasn't rigid either. The church continually protested the wrong of its day and reshaped itself to be relavant to its people and time.

Luther was only in the town of Eisleben a couple times — when he was born and when he died. He probably died of heart failure. In those last moments, he was asked if he wanted to remain steadfast to Christ and the doctrine he had preached. Luther answered with a distinct and clear "Jawohl" — "Yes, indeed!" So may we.

Children's Object Lesson

John Calvin, God's Man

Objects: *a will, a linchpin, and a gift-wrapped box.*

Good morning, boys and girls. I brought three things I'd like to share with you today. They tell us about a saint who shaped the church many years ago. *(Hold up the will, the linchpin, and the gift box.)* Do you know what each of these is?

This is a will. It's something we write to tell other people what to do with our money and possessions when we die. It also tells them how we'd like to be remembered.

The saint we talk about today is John Calvin. He emphasized learning what God's will is for all of us. He reshaped the church into an organization that tries its very best to accomplish God's will in the world. If, through prayer, John Calvin determined God wanted and willed something, he made sure that it was accomplished — even if it took the government to help.

I'll bet not many of you know this is a linchpin. It's used when we pull things from a drawbar on a tractor. The tongue is placed on the drawbar of the tractor. Then this pin is put through. It doesn't let go; it pulls whatever we want along.

John Calvin said that the linchpin of a Christian's life is the Bible. According to Calvin, God's Word is the most important thing to be considered in the church. He shaped his church so that the very linchpin was the Bible — God's word.

And everybody knows that this is a special gift. It's wrapped with gift paper and has a bow. It reminds us of Christmas and our birthdays when we receive special gifts, even if we don't deserve them.

Calvin shaped the church around a God who gives us the gift of being a part of his family and being saved. Like Martin Luther, he taught that we are saved by the lovely gift of Jesus Christ on the cross and that it is entirely a gift from God, because God cares about us.

As we talk about saints who shaped the church and the

special one today, John Calvin, I hope you remember these three things about Calvin. 1) The will reminds us that Calvin wanted most of all to determine what God's will is for us in the world. 2) The linchpin tells us that Calvin built his church around the Bible. 3) The gift reminds us that Calvin taught that we are made part of God's family and saved as a gift from God.

John Calvin, God's Man

Picture a police officer, like Dan Dusenbery* of our congregation, arriving on the porch of Dr. Ralph Dorner* one evening, putting him under arrest, and taking him to the new Polk County jail. Can you imagine his then being taken to the courthouse by prosecutor Dan Johnston* and tried before our church council for heresy because he did not believe as we did? Can you further envision his being found guilty by Judge Leo Oxburger* in spite of attorney Phil Miller's* pleas, brought to Nollen Plaza mid-morning, and hanged for his crime on a gallows constructed by our Neumann Brothers* Construction Company?

We consider today a saint of the church who could, and did, envision such a city government. It all happened in the sixteenth century in Geneva, Switzerland, at the same time Katie Luther was brewing her "Katie beer" in neighboring Wittenberg, Germany.

But I am ahead of my story. John Calvin, sixteen years younger than Martin Luther, was born July 10, 1509, in Noyon, France. He was the second son of a deposed secretary to the bishop.

He studied Augustine, whom we heard about last week, extensively. At age nineteen he received his college degree in law.

In 1533 Calvin joined the Reformation and broke with the Roman Catholic church. He had had a religious experience in which he believed he had received a mission to restore the

*The point of the illustration is that these individuals are all members of the author's large congregation in Des Moines, Iowa.

church to its original purity. He left France for Protestant Basel and there wrote his famous "Institutes of the Christian Religion" in 1536. It gave Protestant beliefs its most systematic formulation.

A friend, Guillaume Farel, persuaded Calvin to visit, and then remain, in Geneva, Switzerland. There Calvin tried a great experiment — the organization of Geneva under rigid and uniform religious discipline.

The government of the city was put into the hands of pastors, elders and deacons, assisted by a court which was a tribunal of morals. The government wielded the penalty of excommunication and had the power of severe punishment for various religious offenses.

Calvin wrote commentaries on the Old Testament and New Testament and a treatis on predestination. His theology is generally accepted in most non-Lutheran Reformed churches.

Calvin and Luther held many beliefs in common with other reformers and renewers of the church. They did disagree on several items, such as:

the meaning of communion,
predestination of the damned,
and subjugation of the state to the church.

After being run out of Geneva once, Calvin was invited back in 1541 and established his religious government.

Let's look first at his ideas on salvation. John Calvin put a very strong emphasis on grace, just like the rest of the reformers did. He rejected the idea that you could earn your salvation. He held up Paul's writings in the book of Romans: "But by the free gift of God's grace all are put right with him through Christ Jesus, who sets them free." (Romans 3:24)

Calvin also saw the Bible as the very linchpin of the Reformation and our own counsel and guide for what we hold as true about God.

Perhaps most important for many, and certainly for me, is Calvin's picture of God as "to be feared." He saw God not only as a friend, but also as mighty and powerful.

I think we need Calvin's emphasis on the respect of our Creator again. We have emphasized God's forgiving love, his friendliness, his pity and mercy so much, that we have almost lost his majesty. It is right and healthy to have this dimension in our relationship to our heavenly Parent.

We just can no longer saunter into his presence, nonchalantly. Rather, we should approach him with respect as one who created it all and could destroy it all just as well. A couple of years ago, when our grandchildren visited us here in Des Moines, my grandson Brian was shouting and running down the center of the aisle of the church. I blocked the aisle and caught him. He was baffled as to why I stopped him and made him be quiet. I used a word that was vogue right then with people his age to explain my actions: "awesome."

Two years later, this fall, I visited my grandsons in Ohio. I asked them how Confirmation was in their home church. Brian looked at me and just used one word. We both understood: "awesome." God's presence is awesome. Calvin helped us see that, and it is good that he did.

I did find it hard to locate a Presbyterian or another Reformed Christian who still holds the Calvinistic view of what has been called "double predestination." Like Luther, Calvin held that God elects or chooses some to be saved. Paul wrote to the Romans: ". . . so those whom God set apart (predestines), he called; and those he called, he put right with himself, and he shared his glory with them." (Romans 8:30) Unlike Luther, he carried that further to say that God also predestines some to damnation.

Our faith teaches us that we do have the choice to say "no" to God, and for *that* reason some are not saved. However, God would like to save everyone!

We read in 1 Timothy 2:4, "This is good and it pleases God our Savior, who wants *everyone* to be saved and to come to know the truth."

Some just will not permit this salvation to take place. They refuse to allow God to choose them. They want to be left alone. Many theologians describe hell as being left alone.

Because God would like to save everyone, we do not give

up on anyone as long as that person is alive. Nor do we put to death people who might change their minds and allow God to select them for eternity with him.

Again, we read in Ephesians: "Because of his love God had already decided that through Jesus Christ he would make us his sons and daughters — this was his pleasure and purpose." (Ephesians 1:5)

You and I become the instruments of the Holy Spirit in the world, not to force our way on others, but to be the ones through whom God coaxes and loves and invites sinners to repent and change their minds. Every person's ministry is to be that tool of God's Spirit who invites, encourages, and sets an example of allowing God's choice to be active and convincing in the life of another.

It certainly is relevant right now to look at what Calvin tried in Geneva, with new right fundamentalists advocating electing people who promise: change in abortion laws, school prayer amendments, tax credits for parochial schools, removing civil rights for gays, and rejection of the Equal Rights Amendment.

This is close to what Calvin tried in Geneva in the 16th century. Calvin was convinced that he, and only he, knew God's will in that town. He saw the government as an instrument to force that will upon everyone else.

As a result, struggle and conflict broke out over doctrinal points. That led to the actual beheading of Jacques Gruet for blasphemy and the burning of Michael Servetus, a Spanish physician, for an antitrinitarian belief.

In Calvin's day in Geneva, the scene I imagined earlier when I began this sermon was very likely.

Our [Lutheran] tradition holds that there ought to be an

institutional separation of the church and the state and that each must be free to perform its essential task under God. We reject any theory which makes dominance of church over state or state over church.

A statement adopted a few years ago by the Lutheran Church in America said that we believe God ordered there be government. In fact, there *must* be. As long as sinners live together, we need government, and sometimes force, to prevent chaos and especially to protect the weak and the minorities.

We believe we should pray for our government and its leaders, encourage responsible citizenship, hold the state accountable, and help it see and understand God's law. We believe we ought to help the state be just and fair and champion human rights of all citizens. That includes those of different sex, age, color, ethnic background, and sexual preference.

We believe the state ought to guarantee religious liberty for all and maintain a wholesome neutrality toward church bodies, recognizing the religious pluralism of our culture.

A Lutheran pastor in a hurry parked his car with a note on the windshield which said, "Have been round the square ten times. I have an appointment. 'Forgive us our trespasses.' " There was a ticket when he came back, and another note: "Have been round the square ten years. If I don't book you, I'll lose my job. 'Lead us not into temptation.' " *(Church Times)*

That is proper interaction of church and state!

It did not work for Calvin in Geneva. It only led to bloodshed and persecution; the same will be true in our age. When one denomination or religious faction tries to force its particular beliefs on the rest by the civil law, it always leads to anarchy. The minority gets trampled. This is not the way God would have us behave or govern ourselves.

Despite ill health for several years, God's man, Calvin, kept up his preaching, teaching, and writing. Eventually, he died in Geneva on May 27, 1564.

The Huguenots were Calvinists, and in 1622, Calvinism became the state religion in Holland. That is why you can drive to Pella, Iowa, today, and see a Reformed Church on almost every corner.

In Scotland, Calvinism found congenial soil, and thus appears today as the Reformed and Presbyterian churches. Calvin's teachings suffered setbacks in the 18th and 19th centuries, but in our lives we have seen them given importance in a living saint who now shapes the church, Karl Barth.

Shortly before his death, Calvin wrote, "Such is pure and genuine religion, namely, confidence in God coupled with serious fear — fear which both includes in it willing reverence and brings along with it such legitimate worship as is prescribed by law." *(Festivals and Commemorations,* Page 209)

Today we remember this saint who shaped the church for his emphasis on:

salvation by grace;
the profound authority of the Scripture for our lives;
the greatness and awesomeness of God;
and, his unsuccessful attempt at establishing his beliefs about God through the civil government.

Truly, John Calvin was God's man.

Children's Object Lesson

John Wesley: Religion of the Heart

Objects: *a big red paper heart and a list of six rules*

Good morning, boys and girls. I have two things I'd like to show you today: this big red paper heart and this list of six rules. Both tell about John Wesley who was a saint who lived a long time ago. They tell how he shaped the church. He taught Christians about having a heart in their religion.

This heart reminds us that we must not only understand about God and being a part of his family, but we must also have a heart.

This means we must learn to feel about our religion as well as think about it. Having a heart in our religion means that we do as Jesus taught us. We hurt when people hurt; we celebrate when people are happy. We feel for their disappointments and their joys and take part in both. That's the way God wants us to be. He gave us a heart. He wants us to be loving, caring people with big hearts like this one. John Wesley was, and he taught us about it.

A long time ago a house was on fire, and the ceilings and walls were about to cave in. The home was owned by Samuel and Suzanna Wesley, who had eight children. All the children got out of the burning house except John. Then they saw him at a window on the second story and heard him scream for help. He was just 5 years old. A neighbor climbed on top of another man's shoulders and asked John to jump. John jumped and was saved from the burning fire. John's mother always talked about how her son had been, "a brand plucked out of the burning." Thus she thought he was a very special boy who would do special things. He really was!

John's parents, Mr. and Mrs. Wesley, were very strict. I brought along a list of the rules they drew up for their eight children to follow in their home. Let me read them to you:

1. If the children confessed their faults, they were not beaten.
2. No sinful action, like lying, playing at church, dis-

obedience, quarreling, or any form of disrespect should ever pass unpunished.

3. No child was ever beaten twice for the same fault.
4. Every single act of obedience was always commended.
5. Children were expected to respect the property of others.
6. Promises were to be strictly observed.

When you were a part of the Wesley family, the rules were strict. However, the Wesleys were always fair. It works well when families live with rules, because the rules help us respect each other as God wants us to do. John Wesley always believed that as he shaped the church, which is called Methodist today.

When you think about John Wesley as a saint who shaped the church, I hope you'll remember him as one who taught us to have a heart in our faith, as one who kept the rules, and as the young man who was snatched out of the fire in order to do special things for God.

John Wesley: Religion of the Heart

His mother was the daughter of an Anglican priest, and his father was an unsuccessful pastor in the Church of England. He had been raised in the parsonage — one of nineteen children.

He, too, became a priest, but he sensed something missing. Religion to this "preacher's kid" seemed cold, cruel, and intellectual.

Then came May 24, 1738. Early in the morning he read in his Bible: "In this way he has given us the very great and precious gifts he promised, so that by means of these gifts you may escape from the destructive lust that is in the world, and may come to share the divine nature." (2 Peter 1:4)

A little later in the morning, Scripture came alive again as he read: "You are not far from the kingdom of God."

In the afternoon, he stopped by St. Paul's and heard the anthem, "Out of the deep have I called unto thee, O Lord: Lord hear my voice . . ."

In his own words we hear what happened next: "In the evening I went very unwillingly to a society in Aldersgate Street, where one was reading Luther's preface to the *Epistle to the Romans.* About a quarter before nine, while he was describing the change which God works in the heart through faith in Christ, I felt my heart strangely warmed. I felt I did trust in Christ, Christ alone for salvation; and an assurance was given me that he had taken away *my* sins, even *mine,* and saved *me* from the law of sin and death." (p. 56 *John Wesley and His World* by John Pudney)

John Benjamin Wesley always pointed back to that day

when his "heart was strangely warmed" as the day he began his ministry and message of Methodism.

Wesley went on to take the Christian faith to the masses of people including the uneducated, the poor, and those in debtors prisons of England. It was a very different approach; it was religion of the heart.

After this conversion experience, he emphasized immediate salvation and taking the faith to simple folk and sinners.

His older brother Charles had been converted about three weeks before this. He wrote nearly 5,000 hymns reflecting this Wesley "heart faith."

John Wesley was truly a saint who shaped the church and gave it heart.

His father, Samuel, the Anglican priest, and his mother, Suzanna, were what were called back then "nonconformists." Suzanna came from a family of 24 or 25 (her father could not remember for sure), and she gave birth to 19 children in 20 years. Nine survived. John was number 15, born June 17, 1703.

The Wesley family lived in severe poverty. The Reverend Samuel Wesley was jailed once for three months for bad debts.

When John was five years old, the parsonage caught fire and "Jacky" was trapped inside. Two neighbor men formed a human ladder to the second-floor window, and John climbed down. That rescue affected the Christian religion around the world. From then on, John Wesley's mother called him "a brand plucked out of the burning." He became the founder of Methodism and profoundly affected the shape of our church.

Mother Suzanna educated the kids. She was a strict disciplinarian. From her, Wesley must have received his methodical way of organizing.

While in college, John started a "Holy Club" for students who wanted to practice the religious life. Methodism points to its origin in those clubs. Wesley developed a set of rules for the best use of one's time:

1. Begin and end every day with God

2. Be diligent in your calling
3. Employ all spare hours in religion
4. Avoid drunkards and busybodies
5. Examine yourself every night
6. Set aside an hour of devotion each day
7. Avoid all manner of passion

After his conversion at Aldersgate, John established Sunday church schools, preached in the fields of England, and was careful never to hold his worship when the Anglican Church did. He remained an Anglican priest almost to the end of his life. He finally broke with the organized church because it refused to ordain several Methodist clergy to go to the United States.

John Wesley ordained them himself in 1784. Francis Asbury became the Wesley of this country. Religion of the heart arrived in the United States. Holy Clubs started by Wesley in Savannah are often referred to as the beginnings of Methodism in America. Francis Asbury especially took that heart religion out into the country.

John Wesley has a lot to teach us Christians in our day. I expect I like him so much because he stressed self-discipline, punctuality, organization, and a heart religion.

I believe we need a good dose of Methodism in our Christian faith today. For some reason some claim it's not good to be a "bleeding heart" or "do-gooder." Yet, that was the very center of Jesus' teaching.

Conversion for Wesley meant taking this exciting life-changing faith out to the cruel, indifferent world. Liturgies, fine vestments, and long-standing traditions were okay, but religion needed a heart — like Christ had demonstrated during his ministry in Palestine. Jesus said we should care for the leper, bind up wounds of the beaten traveler, visit those in prison, care for the children, the poor, and the downtrodden. He claimed we should even love our enemies as much as we love ourselves.

Wesley's general rule of life was, "Whenever you are to

do an action, consider how God did or would do the like, and do imitate his example.''

A week before John Wesley died, he wrote a letter to the young abolitionist William Wilberforce: ''. . . go on, in the name of God and in the power of his might, 'til even American slavery, the vilest that ever saw the sun, shall vanish before it.'' (John Pudney, *John Wesley and His World)*

Religion with a heart will work to bring compassion to people who need it in any age. That would be folks who are AIDS victims. It would be folks like the hungry of our community. Religion with a heart will lobby for the suffering Iowa farmer and those single parents on ADC. You may say ''Not practical.'' Perhaps. You may say ''Not popular.'' You're probably right. But ''Christ-like''? you bet. That it is! And when our hearts are warmed with God's gospel, we must be active, concerned Christians. That means being bleeding hearts, and it means touching the untouchables of our own day. It means rolling up our sleeves and making a difference in their lives.

For very cold weather there are now available hand and feet warmers run by batteries you carry with you. We Christians need heart-warmers so we can feel our religion. These are . . . ''very great and precious gifts he promises us.'' And we, too, . . . ''may come to share the divine nature.'' (1 Peter 1:4)

There was no elitism on Wesley's part once his heart was warmed. He took it out to all of God's people. An R. Hancock completed a famous engraving of John Wesley in 1790. The words over the engraving are ''He went about doing good.'' It ought be said of us as well.

Perhaps we need a conversion. Wesley was the son of a preacher. His mother was the daughter of a preacher. He grew up in the parsonage. He was educated to be a preacher. Still, there was no heart in it! It was stiff, formal, and cold. There was no connection between the words read in the Bible and said during worship and what happened out in the world. Wesley even began to doubt he was saved. He thought he might just be going through intellectual exercises. He feared his faith was not whole-hearted. So this man added to Luther's "justification by grace through faith only" heart and action.

He saw the need to feel religion and do religion as evidence that he was one of God's saved.

Let's consider that. A billboard on a busy avenue here in our city a while back said: "Would you consider preaching what you practice?"

> Does how we treat minorities,
> does what we give in the offering,
> does our language,
> does how we act at home,
> does our attitude here toward other members,
> does how many we have invited into church reflect our religion?

Or, have we completely divorced our worship here from our actions the rest of the time?

It's significant that Wesley wrote in his journal once after his conversion at Aldersgate: "I began to pray with all my might for those who had in a more special manner despitefully used me and persecuted me." (Pudney, page 56)

When Martin Luther was asked about doing good in the community of Wittenberg, where his parish church was located, he told the people that first he would have to make Christians out of the church members before they could go out and do the good things.

We, too, need a better connection from brain to heart in the practice of faith.

It's interesting to all of us to note that John Wesley failed in many aspects of his life. His courtship of three women didn't go well at all. Finally, he married Mrs. Vazeille in 1751. He wasn't a good husband. The marriage ended in separation.

Wesley went to Georgia with Oglethorpe to establish that colony made up of people out of London's debtors prisons. He failed there, too. Wesley wasn't liked, just as his father wasn't liked in his parish years before. Yet, Methodism sees its roots in this country and in those Holy Clubs he started in Savannah, Georgia.

It was in Georgia that Wesley met the Moravians. Peter Boehler and a fellow by the name of Spangenburg profoundly influenced Wesley's spiritual development. They had an inner experience of the Christian faith about which he knew nothing so far. On the voyage across the Atlantic he was greatly impressed at how these Moravians had no fear of death in a storm at sea.

The Church of England saw him as a failure, too. He was banned from preaching in its churches and had to take to the fields and public halls for his congregations. Yet he profoundly influenced the faith of Christians around the world.

John was a failure with family. Brother Samuel Wesley, a good straight-laced and educated Anglican priest, called people like his brother religious fanatics and canting fellows. He thought John had gone dangerously mad.

It is true, isn't it? God can and does use our failures for good purposes. What the world often counts as failure, God works through. He brings great purpose and accomplishment. Those words must have echoed through his heart and head many times: "In this way he has given us the very great and precious gifts he promised...so that you may come to share the divine nature." (2 Peter 1:4)

I like most of all the words Wesley said just before he died. It was March 2, 1791. The man who failed in so many ways, the giant of faith who put heart into our religion even today, the one who "went about doing good," said what became the rallying cry of Methodism and ought to be of all Christianity, even in this hour: "The best of all — God is with us."

Children's Object Lesson

William Booth and His Hallelujah Army

Objects: *a tamborine, a trumpet, and something representing a soldier, like arm stripes.*

Good morning, boys and girls. Perhaps you know what I'm holding up:

This is a tamborine; listen to the noise it makes.
This is a trumpet; it can make a loud sound.
And these are military stripes; they don't make any noise at all.

I show you these three things because they tell us about a saint who shaped the Christian church years ago. His name was William Booth. Mr. Booth grew up under poor circumstances and was a part of the Christian church. It worried him that more wealthy Christians didn't seem to invite the very poor into their churches. Mr. Booth was also concerned that if very poor people came into the wealthy's churches, the poor wouldn't be comfortable and stay very long.

This stripe that goes on a soldier's arm tells us that William Booth organized Christians like an army. He saw us Christians as God's fighting force against the bad, evil, and ugly in the world. Today people who belong to William Booth's church, called the Salvation Army, have names and ranks like military. There are sergeants, corporals, and colonels.

This tamborine reminds us that Mr. Booth thought the music that Christians use should be very simple, have a good beat, and attract uneducated people. The tamborine, which can be played by almost anyone, can sound out a rhythm which expresses joy. The tamborine can also be used to receive offerings in worship, even when worship is held on street corners and other outdoor places.

The trumpet reminds us that music was very important to William Booth's church. The Salvation Army still uses trumpets, accordians, and pianos to attract attention to the Christian faith and to praise God.

The trumpet can also sound advance for military people. It wakes them up and sends them out against the enemy. William Booth saw that as the role of the church on earth. He shaped his church to do that kind of battle. The trumpet is often mentioned in Scripture to announce the Second Coming of Christ and the day when we are judged. William Booth shaped his church to remind people that day was soon. He taught that we ought to get our lives in order so that we will be ready to be received into God's kingdom on judgment day.

Remember this about this saint called William Booth: He shaped the church into an army who fought evil in the world. He introduced a different kind of music for common people. He invited the poor into God's family. And he told us to get ready for Christ's coming again.

William Booth and His Hallelujah Army

In addition to those faithful millions who have prayed, sung, studied the Bible, and witnessed to their faith, there have been a few exceptional saints in every age who have altered the shape and course of the Christian church in their days and in the days to come. These few, through whom the Spirit of God did mighty acts, walked ten feet tall. They were spiritual giants while they lived. They have followed in the footsteps of such as Moses, Jeremiah, Amos, Hosea, Peter, John, and Paul. Their vision for God's people was the greater view, the grander insight, and the wider horizon for his "body alive" called the Christian church.

Through these saints God reached down, and often not so gently shook the very foundation, theology, and organization of his saved in the world. Through them he often stabbed the heart and conscience of his people. Their names are familiar to Christians worldwide:

1. *St. Augustine,* who pointed us to the nature of our sinfulness and God's gift of forgiveness.
2. *John Calvin,* who gave us a sense of being chosen by God.
3. *John Wesley,* who held before us religion of the heart.
4. And today, *William Booth,* founder of the Salvation Army, who placed the cause of the down-and-out before the church.

The Scripture, which reverberates through this man's life and ministry, is from Matthew 22:37-39. "Jesus answered,

'Love the Lord your God with all your heart, with all your soul, and with all your mind...Love your neighbor as you love yourself.' "

Jesus once answered a teacher of the Law who simply asked, ". . . which is the greatest commandment . . . ?" Our Lord responded that we must love God and our neighbor as we love ourselves. When pressed by the people to define who that neighbor is, our Lord replied with the story of the Good Samaritan. He tells us all those who need our help are our neighbors. This includes the poor, the misfits, the elderly, the lonely, and those dregs of society who wander in a stupor up and down the alley by our church.

Perhaps more than any other Christian, William Booth placed them squarely on our conscience.

When asked the secret of his success in the Salvation Army, General William Booth said, "I will tell you the secret. God has had all there was of me. There have been people with greater brains than I, people with greater opportunities. But from the day I got the poor of London on my heart and caught a vision of what Jesus Christ could do with them, on that day I made up my mind that God should have all of William Booth there was. And if there is anything of power in the Salvation Army today, it is because God has had all the adoration of my heart, all the power of my will, and all the influence of my life."

Does that sound familiar? Jesus said, ". . . Love the Lord your God with all your heart, with all your soul, and with all your mind . . . Love your neighbor as yourself." William Booth did just that!

Booth was born April 10, 1829, in Nottingham, England, son of Samuel and Mary Moss Booth.

He lived with his parents in poverty. His father died when William was fourteen. He became an apprentice to a Unitarian pawn broker, who was often the only help that stood between this family and eviction.

He was a tall, pale-faced boy with raven black hair and

flashing eyes. His dad insisted that he and his three sisters attend Methodist worship.

"Willful Will," as he was called, became a Methodist. They got their name by their stern rules of upright conduct, formulated by their founder, John Wesley, whom we heard about last week.

As he describes his conversion, it was rather simple. It was in 1844. He was returning from a Methodist worship service late at night, and simply experienced a "spiritual exultation flooding his whole being." What was extraordinary about that conversion was that he saw the need immediately to change his life, seek out all the people he had wronged, and make amends for those actions.

Now here the story becomes fun for us to consider. Booth got excited with his newfound piety. On a Sunday morning in 1846, he ushered into plush Broad Street Church in Nottingham, people from its "bottoms," a cruel slum of the city.

Before that, if the poor insisted on attending worship, they had to enter by a side door and sit behind a screen so that the well-to-do would not have to be embarrassed by their presence.

Booth was soundly criticized for his boldness of bringing the poor right down front. Nevertheless, he continued and became a Methodist revivalist preacher. He had great success bringing religion to the masses of people. That very success caused considerable jealousy among other Methodist clergy.

In 1861, he left the Methodists because of their unwillingness to let him reach out with the Gospel to all sorts of people. The reasons he gave for leaving the Methodist organization were three:

1. The poor and down-and-out would not go where he sent them.
2. They were not wanted when they did go.
3. He soon discovered that he wanted them to assist him in winning others who were of their station in life.

So, he began his own movement that year. It was called "The Christian Mission," and worked in the areas of evangelism, social ministry, and rescue work.

Christian Mission was later renamed and officially began as "The Salvation Army" in 1865. From that time on, Booth spent much time traveling and addressing meetings of his "Hallelujah Army," which soon spread to Australia, Europe, and the United States.

While some of us are uneasy about using military terms in the church, Booth loved the military as a child and so appropriated these terms for his new organization. The "local unit" became a corps working from a citadel. "Knee drill" stood for prayer. "Fire a volley" meant to shout "Hallelujah!" "Fix bayonets" meant to raise your right hand in public declaration. And Salvationists did not die; they were simply "promoted to glory."

That is William Booth, a man who took seriously our Lord's command to "love our neighbor as we love ourselves." He truly shaped the church.

I think William Booth and his "Hallelujah Army" have a lot to teach Christians, especially us Christians who have succeeded economically.

He certainly did hold before us the fact that the poor have God's special attention and concern. He took the Scripture seriously and literally, and that was a shock to the good Christians around him. Things have not changed much, have they?

The Scripture is full of admonitions to help and to be deeply concerned for the poor of our day. Jesus set an example in his own ministry, too. He reached out and tried to help:

- the blind Bartimaeus of Jericho,
- the ill at Pool Bethesda,
- the hungry of Galilee's shore,
- the illiterate up by Tyre and Sidon,
- the prostitute of Bethany's streets.

I would like to share with you my deep concern that, especially for us who gather in this church, we have all but ignored religion for such as these.

We have built our beautiful sanctuaries, composed our

liturgies and developed our worship customs, and so educated and sophisticated our clergy, that we easily make the poor downright uncomfortable to be around us. When those who stink and are unshaven and disheveled try to join us in our worship, the glares soon drive them away.

Jesus said, ". . . Love your neighbor as you love yourself."

Trouble is, we can be so insulated in our skywalks, plush working areas, beautiful neighborhoods, and air-conditioned cars on four-lane freeways, that we do not even know that these unfortunate exist.

Perhaps the only excuse for our existence in "a ghetto of the middle and upper class" is that we also need God's salvation, and we need desperately to be rescued from our greed and selfishness.

Should we not be the Samaritan along Jerusalem to Jericho who helps the beaten and left-for-dead poor of our day?

Oh, how we need to keep them on our hearts and make a difference in their lives. How we need legislators and leaders of the country who can make a difference also, and who will open their eyes to see the poor, instead of denying their very existence.

William Booth, with all his military nomenclature, would certainly hold before our conscience today the priorities of continuing to pile up more and more exotic and nuclear weapons, and spending billions and billions of borrowed dollars on them while cutting those few programs which aid the unfortunate, the poor, and the elderly.

William Booth would hug you for your generous support of the Lutheran Church in America's World Hunger Appeal. He would love you to death for your support of Bethel and Door of Faith Missions. He would rejoice when we would risk entering into any kind of jail ministry. He would give thanks for that small group of Christians in our congregation who are working desperately to build housing for the hearing-impaired, the handicapped, and the elderly.

You see, that Scripture, through William Booth, became

hands and feet and heart to other people. "Love the Lord your God with all your heart, with all your soul, and with all your mind...and your neighbor as yourself."

While his concern for the poor and oppressed was by far the major emphasis of his ministry, I think perhaps the greatest thing he taught us is that no one is ever beyond the help, concern, and care of God. A person can never reach such a low state of being that God gives up.

There are also some other interesting things about William Booth: he supported the idea of women clergy long before most people even thought of it.

William married Catherine Mumford in 1855. They had a number of children, all who eventually took leadership roles in the Salvation Army.

Once, on a Sunday morning, when Catherine was dutifully listening to her husband hold forth from the pulpit, she got out of her pew, came down the center aisle, tugged at his elbow in the pupit, and remarked, "William, sit down now. I have something to say." She gave a magnificent sermon. All the time Booth was thinking. When her address was over, he instructed the congregation to be sure to come back that evening and hear his wife preach. Thus began years and years of an effective team ministry — a woman and a man in the pulpit.

Catherine Mumford Booth later said, "O prejudice, what will it not do! . . . That woman is in any respect except physical strength . . . inferior to man I cannot see cause to believe, and I am sure no one can prove it from the word of God." *(The General Next to God,* by Richard Collier)

About the time Amelia Jenks Bloomer of Council Bluffs, Iowa, was calling for women's suffrage, Catherine Booth of London was calling for women to occupy the pulpits of our churches.

The Booths had quite an influence on the use of music as part of evangelistic services. In 1878, William hired three people to play brass just to accompany hymns, and thus the first Salvation Army band was born. Interesting it is that, like Martin

Luther, Booth took popular tunes and gave them Christian lyrics. The music for "Storm the fort of darkness, bring them down" was first "Here's to good old whiskey." Booth is quoted as saying, "Why should the devil have all the best tunes?"

It is inspiring to read about the lives of Catherine and William Booth. They lived out their Christianity. A consistency existed between what they said they believed at church and how they lived and treated each other at home. It is easy to give "mixed signals" to those with whom we share our home. And yet, all the attributes we admire in Jesus on Sunday we ought to practice on Monday: kindness, love of enemy, concern for the poor, sharing with others, gentleness and patience with the other person.

I was moved to tears when I read these words: "Daughter Evangeline once said of her mom and dad, 'My parents did not have to say a word to me about Christianity. I saw it in action.' "

Catherine once told her daughter Kate: "You are not in the world for yourself. You have been sent for others. The world is waiting for you." *(The General Next to God,* by Richard Collier)

How we can *all* improve on this area of our discipleship!

Every once in a great while a sensitive saint comes along who takes it all to heart more than the rest of us. That person pierces our conscience, for we see in that person how God would really like us to be. So it is with William Booth and his "Hallelujah Army."

A Salvationist visiting Nottingham Chapel, where William Booth was converted, kneeled near the commemorative tablet and prayed, "O God, do it again! Do it again." My prayer is the same today: "Do it again, God, do it again!"

Children's Object Lesson

Mother Teresa and the Dying Poor

Object: *a picture of Mother Teresa*

Today, boys and girls, we will talk about the life of a very special living saint who is still shaping the church. Her name is Mother Teresa. I brought a picture of her today so you could see what she looks like.

Mother Teresa is now over 75 years old. She was named after Saint Teresa of Avilia who lived about 500 years ago. Saint Teresa of Avilia taught many faithful church people about prayer. We can put our hands like this *(fold hands)* because of Teresa of Avilia. We remember that she was able to teach many about meditation and prayer as a nun in the Roman Catholic Church.

There are other ways we can use our hands that God doesn't like nearly as well. *(Make a fist.)* We can hit people with hate. *(Point with a finger.)* We can blame people for things that are wrong and call names. *(Put hand on shoulder.)* Or we can reach out and offer to help people who are in trouble. *(Open hand facing up.)* And we can offer to do what we can for people who have special needs. Teresa of Avilia, after whom Mother Teresa was named, liked best to fold her hands to pray. Mother Teresa does too.

Wherever Mother Teresa speaks to Christians, she shows them her hand like this *(hold up the back of the hand with fingers and thumb extended)* and tells them that thumb and fingers actually mean these five words: "you, do, this, for, me."

First, this saint who shapes the church folds her hands and prays to God. Then she goes out to answer other people's prayers with those same hands.

Christians around the world love Mother Teresa because she answers so many people's prayers. The people are hungry, sick, and dying. She sees that the way to answer prayer is to be the hands of God in other people's lives.

I think she's probably called mother because mothers care

about their children. Mothers are always there when we need to be comforted, we are frightened, or we're about to do something we shouldn't do. Mother Teresa is like that.

I hope you can remember Mother Teresa. You'll often see her on television news reports.

She is so wonderful because first she folds her hands like this and prays to God. Then she sees that hand with each finger representing: "you — do — this — for — me."

Let's pray today in church. Then let's do something for God and be his hands in the world this afternoon.

Mother Teresa and the Dying Poor

Jesus took his closest followers up on the side of a mountain for a spiritual retreat. There he tried to teach them about Christianity. One of the great promises he gave them was, "Blessed are the merciful, for they shall obtain mercy." (Matthew 5:7)

Seventy-six-year-old Mother Teresa of India knows what Jesus meant. She knows it like few people have understood since he first said it.

Not long ago this tiny wisp of tough gentleness, who won the Nobel Peace prize, visited Norristown, Pennsylvania. There she helped dedicate a convent which now offers shelter to the poor in a neighborhood where such missions are prohibited. As a part of that dedication at Saint Patrick's Roman Catholic Church, Mother Teresa urged all her followers to "share the joy of loving."

That must be what Jesus meant when he sat down on the hillside and said, "Blessed are the merciful, for they shall obtain mercy."

If your life lacks a certain joy;
if you don't experience the kind of return on your religion
you think you ought —
listen further.

Something leaps out at me when I study the lives of the saints who shaped the church. The more spiritual they were, the closer they allowed God to come to them; and the more their lives were permeated with the Spirit, the more the poor and down-and-out were on their conscience. The more they rolled up their sleeves to help, the more they felt a certain joy and peace in their own lives.

We have already seen that in the lives of St. Augustine, St. Francis of Assisi, and William Booth, founder of the Salvation Army. I have seen it with my own eyes in only a few people whom I have ever known. One of those people was Dom Helder Camara, a Roman Catholic bishop and champion of the poor in Brazil. "Blessed are the merciful, for they shall obtain mercy."

In her diary Mother Teresa wrote: "Friday. Talked to X who had said he had come to school on an empty stomach. They have nothing to eat at home. I gave him the money for my bus fare to buy some food, and walked home in the evening." (Epilogue, *Mother Teresa, Her People and Her Work)*

In Calcutta, India, not so far from the place where Indira Ghandi was assassinated recently, is a shrine under a tree where you will find three people revered: Jesus, the Virgin Mary, and Mother Teresa! The nuns are embarassed by this, and yet it measures how those East Indians, and indeed, Christians all over the world, see this humble little woman as one of the greatest of living saints. Jesus said, "Blessed are the merciful, for they shall obtain mercy."

Let's look at her life briefly and then see what that life has to say to us who attend this worship service today.

Born Agnes Bejaxhire in 1910 of Albanian parents, at Skopje, Yugoslavia, she had a sister and a brother. In 1928, she went to Loretto Abbey in Dublin, Ireland, and from there to India to begin her training to be a nun.

Mother Teresa taught school in Calcutta. Her final vows were said in 1937. In 1946, while on a train, Mother Teresa heard the call of God. She requested permission from her superior to live outside the cloister and to work in the Calcutta slums. She took training as a nurse and opened her first slum school in Moti Jheel in 1948.

In 1950, the new congregation of the Missionaries of Charity was approved and instituted in Calcutta, and from there spread through India. Since then she has opened centers for the poor all over the world in such places as Caracas, Colombo, Rome, and Amman. In this country her mission centers to the poor include the Bronx and Norristown, Pennsylvania.

She is known worldwide and received the Nobel Peace prize in 1979. (She asked that instead of the usual formal banquet and monetary gift, they let her use the money for the poor. Thus she fed 15,000 of Calcutta's hungry.)

Mother Teresa's Missionaries of Charity have collected thou sands of abandoned and dying people from the streets, helping them to die with dignity, peace, and above all else, love. Her own arms have embraced the lepers, misfits, poor, and those hot and ravished with contagious disease.

She is a living saint of our day who has shaped, and is still shaping, the church. She knows the truth of Jesus' promise, "Blessed are the merciful, for they shall obtain mercy."

We have much to learn from this living saint about how God is, and how he wants us to treat each other and those out in the world. Here is the patron saint of us who are pleased to be called "do-gooders" and "bleeding hearts."

Something about Mother Teresa's life and the lives of her Missionaries of Charity is personally attractive to us. It breaks through all the plastic and artificial elements of our own existence. It somehow removes from our faces the mask of pretention we often wear. She teaches us that a deeper spiritual relationship with God is possible in all our lives, and that it often comes from helping others in his name.

We do recall that Jesus promised, if we give a cup of cold water to a thirsty person, we are actually giving it to our Lord.

My own life is so inconsistent in this area. I'll bet yours is, too. We live "high on the hog" here in the United States, compared with others around the world. And, it does not bring the satisfaction to our lives that we all long for. Yet, this is a time when our newspaper announces 35 million are starving in Africa, with Ethiopia estimating six to seven million people in danger of dying by starvation. In a day when our military boasts it can put a strike force anywhere in the world within a few hours, we find that large amounts of food, help for those hungry, rot on the docks of Africa's ports.

Here is a woman who lives so humbly and resists all the traps of wealth that Jesus warned us against. Here is a woman who seems so at peace and content with her life. Her lifestyle so blesses her existence.

Prayer seems to be the center or focus of her and her missionaries' lives. A little book for children about Mother Teresa* tells how they rise at 4:30 a.m. for prayers and meditation, followed by Mass. After Mass they do their washing and other chores. Mother Teresa often cleans the toilets. They are allowed no possessions, just two saris, a crucifix, a pair of sandals, and some prayer books — strikingly familiar equipment to that which Jesus gave the seventy when he sent them out on their missionary journey.

After the morning chores they go out into the slums of their city to the dying, the lepers, and the abandoned of every age, including murderers. Here they seem to experience best the joy of loving.

Perhaps Mother Teresa illustrates where we also can find satisfaction for our lives. It rests in humility, sharing, and serving those who do not deserve it. It is in having mercy.

Think of the implications for stewardship. We who have chosen the much-more-difficult way, according to Jesus — that is, to surround ourselves with possessions and money — ought, for our own spiritual safety, to consider a radical change in our priorities. Certainly all of us ought to be giving more than the minimal ten percent tithe that is called for in the Scripture!

Genevieve Winston of Clarksburg, West Virginia, wrote this paragraph to *The Lutheran* magazine: "Knowing that my son might raid the refrigerator, I put a sign on the cover of a freshly baked pie stating simply: 'Church pie.' When I went to take it to church I was surprised to see these words written under my message: 'Lord, have mercy.' " Jesus said, "Happy

---

**Mother Teresa*, by Anne Sebba, Julia MacRae Books © 1982, New York.

are those who are merciful to others, God will be merciful to them."

Mother Teresa has a lot to teach us about humility, too. Often we are proud and arrogant, even when worshiping and serving the Christ. We refuse the menial task. Our feelings get hurt if we are not recognized and thanked for what we do. We have to "have it our way," like Burger King promises.

In Mother Teresa we see the great persuasive power of humility. She does not lead with her chin. She leads with her heart, and thus knows the joy of loving and being loved.

And, oh, what living proof she is for the fact that our deeds speak so much louder than our words.

In the October, 1984, issue of *The World Times* we read where Mother Teresa said,

> *Women are the heart of the world and would be better priests than men . . . No man can even come close to the love and compassion a woman is capable of giving. A woman priest will perform and her message will percolate down to the roots . . .*

Maybe Mother Teresa has something there. Maybe that is why our own male-dominated church has been so slow to help very many and so careful to take care of itself first. Perhaps the male ego has gotten in the way.

Most of all, Mother Teresa pointed to the dying poor who needed to be comforted and loved. Let us remember Jesus' promise that "Happy are those who mourn, God will comfort them." We ought to take seriously what it means for a Christian to die.

Recently I came through O'Hare Airport and noticed a big red arrow sign with the word "Terminal" above it. Everyone was going that direction without questioning. Perhaps we need to take seriously the truth that we are all terminal and that we are all going to die. Because this life that we know here does not go on forever, we ought to live differently.

Yet, death need not be something we fear for we who are

the saved, a part of God's family. We know we have a place prepared for us. We know we have a God who loves us. We know we have a Savior who worked forgiveness for us on the cross. We know we have an Easter resurrection that is the model of how it will be for us also.

During a recent visit to the hospital, I came upon George, who had not attended this church for years but still considered himself to be a member. He was a crusty old codger. I had never seen him before. I shook his arm to wake him in the hospital bed. He opened his eyes, saw me there in clerical collar and black suit, and exclaimed, "Am I that bad?"

It *is* that bad. We *will* die, but we will also *live* again — and forever. The Scripture assures us there is a new Jerusalem waiting for us and our names are in the book of life. We know that when we mourn we will be comforted.

When people are dying, the Holy Spirit wants desperately to work through the doctors, medical health teams, hospitals, hospice personnel, pastors, church members, spouses, and family so they might die unafraid, with dignity, and especially knowing they are loved.

We Christians must address the whole subject of medical ethics because we now live in a time when the heart of a baboon can be transplanted into a little Baby Fay in California.

We need to ask when, and if, the machines of intensive care ought to be turned off. We need to ask how to be truthful in relationships with dying patients, and how to not only attempt to cure disease and repair injury, but also care about relating to the patient as a person. We need to discover ways life can be lived to the fullest until death occurs. We need to explore how one decides the dilemma between quantity of life and quality of life.

Mother Teresa would agree with our church that, above all, hope and meaning in life are possible, even in times of suffering and adversity. This is a truth powerfully proclaimed in the resurrection faith of our church.

That is our saint for today — Mother Teresa, concerned about the dying poor.

Musical Notes

Music for worship should always be chosen with care. Congregations may not seem to notice when hymns and anthems have little to do with Scripture readings, prayers, and the sermon. If each item is pleasant on its own, few people may mind if they make no sense together. On the other hand, when the sermon, Scripture readings, prayers, hymns, organ music, choral numbers, and solos do work together, the impact of the whole is much greater.

The music suggested here for these sermons is just a starting point. Many additional selections would work as well, and your own choral library and hymnals are the place to begin.

You may wish to have a theme hymn that you sing each Sunday of the series. One possibility would be "For All Your Saints, O Lord" by Richard Mant (1776-1848), but a number of hymns from the "All Saints" or "Servants of God" section would do. If someone in your congregation is a writer perhaps that person could create a stanza for each reformer to fit the hymn, "By All Your Saints in Warfare" (#177 in the *Lutheran Book of Worship*). Look also at "Rise, O Children of Salvation" (*Lutheran Book of Worship* #182).

Solos appropriate for any Sunday of this series include the following:

• "Come, Pure Hearts, in Sweetest Measure" is a Latin sequence hymn translated by Robert Campbell in 1850 and set to music by Ned Rorem. It can be found either in *Hymns III,* published by The Church Hymnal Corporation, or *Ecumenical Praise,* published by Agape.

• "O Jesus, Son of God" (Camille Saint-Saens).

• Phillip Landgrave's piece, "Who Will Go," published by Hope (© 1970), could be either a solo or unison anthem. The text goes beyond a look at a historical figure and asks "What is God asking of me?"

• An anthem for children's choir is "I Sing a Song of the Saints of God" by Lesbia Scott and John H. Hopkins, which can be found in *Choirbook for Saints and Singers,* edited by Carlton Young for Agape. The same text is set by Jane Marshall and is published by Choristers Guild, #A-48, for unison choir with descant. Jane Marshall also provides us with an anthem for adult choir; "He Comes to Us," published by Carl Fischer, CM6996, is a setting of a portion of Albert Schweitzer's "The Quest for the Historical Jesus" (SATB with organ accompaniment).

For more ideas, check your hymnal's topical index under subjects such as commitment, servanthood, saints, witness, and discipleship.

Music for "Augustine, Defender of the Faith"

If music exists which is directly related to St. Augustine, I am not aware of it. One could find music used by Augustinians, but that is probably not the way to proceed. The sermon gives us three teachings about Augustine which will help us in our selection of music:

1. Sin is the result of free will and imperfection.
2. Evil does not stop at the church doors.
3. As a member of the human race, it is only by God's grace that we are saved.

The hymn, "Amazing Grace," by John Newton (1725-1807), immediately comes to mind and would be appropriate. Other hymns about grace would work as well. These include "Give to Our God Immortal Praise!" by Isaac Watts (1674-1748), "Praise, My Soul, the King of Heaven" by Henry F. Lyte (1793-1847), and "There's a Wideness in God's Mercy" by Frederick W. Faber (1814-1863).

The subject of our sinful nature is addressed in a wonderful new hymn, "In Adam We Have All been One" (*Lutheran Book of Worship* #372), by Martin Franzmann (1907-1976).

Appropriate anthems include "Turn Thy Face from My Sins" by Thomas Attwood (1765-1838), published by The Royal School of Church Music, and similar anthems in your Lenten file asking for mercy. A more upbeat anthem is "All His Mercies Shall Endure," from "The Occasional Oratorio" by Handel, edited by Don Malin and published by Belwin Mills.

Music for "St. Francis of Assisi"

Music for St. Francis is both simple and a bit tricky. Simple because certain pieces are obvious, and tricky because some choices would depend on what aspects of this multifaceted saint will be emphasized in the service.

One would expect any service celebrating St. Francis to include the hymn "All Creatures of Our God and King," Henry Draper's paraphrase of Francis' "Canticle of the Sun, and Hymn of Creation." The text is faithful to Francis' interest in all of God's creation.

The other obvious text is the Prayer of St. Francis, "Lord, make me and instrument of thy peace." While probably not by Francis, this poem expresses well his interest in peace and certainly describes the kind of life led by this great man. Almost any publisher's catalogue will list a setting of this text. One I recommend is by David A. Gerig and published by Schmitt, Hall & McCreary (SCHCH 7046). The text is difficult to set well because of the short phrases and rapid changes of thought and mood. Also, it is difficult for music to add anything to this poem that a simple reading won't deliver. Still, the Gerig setting does pretty well.

From there, the choices become more diverse. Should one focus on Francis' quest for peace, a number of hymns suggest themselves:

"God the Omnipotent!"
"O God of Every Nation"
"O God of Love, O King of Peace"

Francis' interest in creation, nature and ecology bring to mind:

"The Beauty of the Earth"
"This Is My Father's World"
"Let All Things Now Living"
"Earth and All Stars"

Servanthood is an obvious theme of this saint's life and I suggest the following:

"God Whose Giving Knows No Ending"
"Lord, Whose Love in Humble Service"
"Love Consecrates the Humblest Act"
"O Master, Let Me Walk with You"

G.I.A. publishes a book "The Praises of God" with choral compositions based on Scritpure and writings of St. Francis, with music by Robert Hutchacher. There is also a recording.

Even after 800 years, this saint continues to inspire us, and whatever music is chosen should glorify God and lift the hearts of those gathered in worship. St. Francis would certainly have wanted a Christ-centered celebration.

Music for "Martin Luther — The Shape of Grace"

In Martin Luther, we have a reformer who wrote both words and music. Involving the congregation in the liturgy through hymn singing was a cornerstone of both his reform of worship practices and his efforts to educate the laity. And, as Marilyn Stulken points out in her *Hymnal Companion to the Lutheran Book of Worship,* " . . . Luther viewed the congregational hymn or chorale as an integral and vital part of the *liturgy,* not merely a general Christian song loosely attached to worship." (Page 19)

Luther's hymns and those of his contemporaries and supporters were often adaptations of older chants from the Offices of the Mass. Sometimes they adapted popular religious songs of the people. Although Luther was a conservative and a child of his times, his music may seem strange and ancient to many, especially to non-Lutherans.

If you do not use the sermons in this book in strict chronological order, Reformation Sunday is an appropriate time to focus on Luther. Surely one would want to use his most famous hymn, "A Mighty Fortress is Our God." If you have not yet tried to sing this tune the way Luther wrote it, consider having the choir sing one stanza in Luther's more rhythmically sophisticated style, and let the congregation sing the version they know on the other verses. Both can be found in the *Lutheran Book of Worship,* Numbers 228 and 229.

"Lord, Keep Us Steadfast in Your Word" (*Lutheran Book of Worship* #230) not only has a text by Luther, but is a strong statement characteristic of his primary beliefs. Rather than singing it in the "four-square" fashion given in the *Lutheran Book of Worship,* try singing it in a freer chant style and adding handbells in this manner: change the half notes that start each phrase to quarter notes, preceded by a rest. Ring two bells, E and B, on each rest, and then sing the phrases in a smooth, speech-rhythm style. If the choir models the first stanza, the congregation will have no trouble following.

Do you have members who play recorders? As instruments dating from Luther's time (he played the recorder as well as the lute), they would add authenticity, as well as the lighter touch we so often miss. It's amazing how much more inviting and joyful a hymn such as "Dear Christians, One and All" (*Lutheran Book of Worship* #299) becomes when introduced by recorders. If the hymn is unfamiliar to your congregation, let the choir sing the first two stanzas with a light organ registration (or with recorders and strings if you have them). Adding brass on the later stanzas not only lends variety to this lengthy hymn, it helps celebrate the fact that Luther saw music as a gift from God and welcomed instruments, as well as voices, in worship.

Of course, anthems and cantatas based on Luther's chorales are easy to find. "Grant Us Thy Peace" by Mendelssohn (H. W. Grey Pub. CMR 1633) is based on a stanza from "Lord, Keep Us Steadfast in Thy Word." A more complete setting of that hymn by Dietrich Buxtehude (1637-1707) is published by Concordia (97-6331). Don't overlook the concertato setting of "A Mighty Fortress" by Drummond Wolff, also published by Concordia (98-2606).

Music for "John Calvin, God's Man"

Music for a service which features the founder of the Reformed tradition offers interesting considerations: should one use the organ, choir, chanted psalms, or "hymns of human composure," when Calvin approved of none of these? Should only unaccompanied singing of metrical psalms take place? In some situations this could be tried with positive results. In other places such an experiment might lead to the public stoning of the parish musician.

It is not necessary to take such a radical approach, however. One might use the hymn tunes of Louis Bourgeois (c.1510-1561). For fifteen years, beginning in 1542, Calvin entrusted Bourgeois with writing and arranging music for the French psalters. "All People That on Earth Do Dwell," to the tune Old Hundreth, is one example of his hymn tunes from the Genevan psalter of 1551. One could explore, as well, the metrical psalms of the English and Scottish Calvinists. An example is "Almighty God, Your Word Is Cast" to St. Flavian. Published first in John Day's psalter of 1562, this tune is in the typical Common Meter with lines of eight syllables alternating with those of six syllables.

One might try "lining out" one of these metrical psalms, using a leader to sing a line which is repeated by the congregation. This was done in many Reformed churches.

Music for "John Wesley, Religion of the Heart"

With John Wesley and the Methodists we have a tradition rich in wonderful, familiar hymns. John Wesley himself wrote hymns and translated many more, including "Jesus, Your Blood and Righteousness," from a German Moravian hymn by Nicolaus Ludvig von Zinzendorf (1700-1760).

By far the more prolific and popular hymn writer was John's brother, Charles Wesley (1707-1788). Charles wrote over 6,000 hymns, many which are among the best and most loved in the English language. "Hark! The Herald Angels Sing," "Christ the Lord is Risen Today," "Jesus Christ is Risen Today," "Rejoice the Lord is King," "You Servants of God, Your Master Proclaim," and "Christ, Whose Glory Fills the Skies" are just a few of his famous productions. With little doubt hymns sung vigorously by the whole congregation should form the backbone of music for a service recognizing John Wesley's contribution to the faith.

But obviously thousands of hymns by the Wesleys exist that are not commonly known. Some of these might provide choir or solo selections. The collection *Ecumenical Praise,* published by Agape (© 1977), has a number of fresh and fascinating examples. Numbers 29 through 34 in the anthology belong to Charles Wesley. They include "Eternal Beam of Light Divine," appropriate for communion or funeral; "Come, O Thou Traveler," containing the powerful, yet personal imagery of Jacob wrestling with the angel. "Open, Lord, My Inward Ear"; and "Rejoice, the Lord is King," set to a tune by Handel, as well as upbeat settings of "Ye Servants of God" and "Christ, Whose Glory Fills the Skies."

The organist will have no trouble finding voluntaries based on Wesley hymns, but one might consider including anthems or organ music by Samuel Sebastian Wesley to show how far the genius of this family extends.

Music for "William Booth and His Hallelujah Army"

Some musicians will have lots of fun planning the music for this Sunday, while others may struggle with it. Music was once again an important tool in the ministry of William Booth. Because of the circumstances in which he worked, the people to which he was appealing, and resources at hand, the style of music which he used was not what most of us typically use in Sunday morning worship. The hymnals of most major denominations just do not contain the street corner revival songs. However, you may wish to secure authentic Salvation Army hymnals or get permission to make legal copies of some songs.

If the Salvation Army Corps in your area has a band or group of singers, you could invite them to provide the special music. If they are not available or you wish to give your own singers the fun of doing some different music, there are at least two additional thematic directions you can take with the music: the imagery of God's people as an army and a social ministry emphasis consistent with Booth's objectives. Hymns that make use of military metaphors include "Onward, Christian Soldiers," "Fight the Good Fight," "The Battle Hymn of the Republic," and "Stand Up, Stand Up for Jesus." An excellent arrangement of this last hymn is available for unison choir with accompaniment for keyboard, piccolo, and snare drum, by Melinda and Greg Ramseth in *Take A Hymn* (Betty Ann Ramseth, Augsburg, 11-2172). Anthem arrangements of the other hymns abound as well.

The other approach would be emphasizing social and justice issues in the selection of music. "All Who Love and Serve Your City" by Erik Routley (1917-1983), "Lord of All Nations, Grant Me Grace" by Olive Wise Spannaus (1916-), "Lord, Whose Love in Humble Service" by Albert F. Bayly (1901-), "O Jesus Christ, May Grateful Hymns be Rising" by Bradford G. Webster (1898-), and "The Church of Christ, in Every Age" by F. Pratt Green (1903-) all are appropriate but may be unfamiliar to the congregation.

One suggestion for a unison anthem or solo would be "We Meet You, O Christ," with text by Fred Kaan and music by Erik Routley. The text makes clear that Christ is found in people in all stations and conditions. It can be found in *Ecumenical Praise.*

Of course, the two approaches are not mutually exclusive and can be mixed. If brass and percussion players are available, this is the Sunday to put them to work!

Music for "Mother Teresa, A Saint for the Dying Poor"

If Reformation Sunday is an appropriate time to remember Martin Luther, then All Saints Sunday would be a good Sunday to remember Mother Teresa. Her work among the dying sends us to search for hymn and anthem texts dealing with serving the poor and working for justice, as well as the All Saints hymns.

Perhaps the most appropriate hymn would be "Lord, Whose Love in Humble Service" (*Lutheran Book of Worship* #423) by Albert F. Bayle. Sung after the sermon, it should carry a lot of weight, if done in a simple, straight-forward style.

"Feed My Lambs" by Natalie Sleeth for unison choir and two flutes reminds us of Christ's commission to serve and care for others.

As we end this series the hope is that the congregation will think in terms of modeling to some extent the lives of these saints. Perhaps Fred Pratt Green's hymn, "How Clear Is Our Vocation, Lord," would express most clearly what we have been trying to convey. It can be found in *Hymnal Supplement,* ©1984 by Agape. The third stanza states:

We marvel how your saints become
in hindrances more sure;
Whose joyful virtues put to shame
the casual way we wear your name,
And by our faults obscure
your power to cleanse and cure.

Amen!